The ABCs of Consulting

Written by Raamin Mostaghimi and Varun Bhartia

Illustrated by Kyle Navaluna

For every Associate who has ever pulled an all-nighter to fix a footnote on a slide that ended up getting cut from the final readout deck

Copyright © 2018 Very Young Professionals Publishing
www.veryyoungprofessionals.com
2nd edition

All rights reserved

ISBN-13:
978-1-7325217-0-4

Your Case Team

A is for **at-risk fees**

When you need to show your clients you've got skin in the game, you can propose **at-risk fees** - that way if your clients don't make money, you're sad too

B is for **back of the envelope**

When you don't actually have real information but you need a recommendation fast, your partner might ask you to do a **back of the envelope** analysis - it sounds better than "guess".

C is for **carry-on luggage**

Checking luggage every time you fly is a real drag - better get some **carry-on luggage** and put it in the overhead compartment instead!

D is for **delegate**

When your partner doesn't want to do something, they can **delegate** the work down to you. Hopefully you can **delegate** the work down to your own Analyst…

E is for **elevator pitch**

When your client's CEO runs into you and only has 30 seconds to talk about your project, you better have your **elevator pitch** ready!

F is for **footnote**

Even though nobody ever reads them, it's important to get every single one of the **footnotes** at the bottom of your slides exactly right!

G is for **guesstimate**

When you totally made up an answer but you want it to sound a little more scientific, you might say you've made a **guesstimate.**

H is for **hotel**

Every week when they're away from home, consultants will sleep, eat, exercise, and even watch TV at a **hotel** - and all while working their tails off!

I is for **impact**

If you don't regularly measure the **impact** your project has, your clients may wonder why they hired you in the first place.

J is for **junior partner**

They don't always know exactly what they want, but **junior partners** are always positive that they want it <u>now</u>. Wait a few years, they'll get the hang of things.

K is for **key**

If you want to make something sound important, just put the word **key** in front of it and presto - problem solved!

L is for **loyalty program**

If you're going somewhere new and you're not sure which hotel to stay at or which airline to fly, just pick the one with your favorite **loyalty program**!

M is for MBA

Business school is a magical place where fully-grown men and women can pretend they are college freshmen again. If they make it through two full years, they get an **MBA**, and they get to talk about it nonstop for the rest of their careers!

N is for **networking**

Nobody is really sure what it means, but **networking** is supposedly the way all real business gets done.

O is for **on the beach**

When a consultant isn't working on a project and gets to stay home and relax (or maybe get pulled onto fourteen proposals all at the same time), they're **on the beach.**

P is for **push back**

When partners ask for fifteen hours of work in the next hour, good consultants will learn to tactfully **push back**. Bad consultants will just make their analysts do it.

Q is for quick-and-dirty

When you agreed to do that fifteen hours of work in under an hour, all you'll have time for is the **quick-and-dirty** version of the output.

R is for **Request for Proposals (RFP)**

When a client has a piece of work to do, and they want a bunch of consultants to fight amongst themselves and give crazy discounts, they'll post an **RFP** and hope for the best.

S is for **slide deck**

Some people make cars for a living. Other people make art. Consultants make **slide decks**, and that's okay too.

T is for **tummy rumble**

When you want to tell your partner that something's wrong, but you want to make it sound not quite so bad, just call it a **tummy rumble**!

U is for **urgent**

When a client asks for anything at all, your junior partner will always tell you it is **urgent** - sometimes even in all caps! Don't worry, it usually isn't.

V is for **value-add**

Before starting on any task, always ask whether it is **value-add** or just make-work. You'll probably have to do it regardless, but it's good to be in the right mindset before you start.

W is for **work-life balance**

When your partner lets you sign offline Thursday night at 9pm, it's so they can pretend they are champions of **work-life balance**.

X is for eXpense report

They're supposed to be super easy if you do them at the end of each week, but somehow you always push off doing your **expense reports** until you've got a four-month backlog and it takes six hours to all get your money back.

Y is for Y-UP

If you really want to book first class but you need your finance department to think you're booking coach, you book **Y-UP**.

Z is for **zebra**

If you hear hoofbeats coming in the distance and you think **zebras** - you're making things too complicated!

Thank you for reading!

Now that you've read this far, you know how to be a consultant!

Looking to become a different kind of Very Young Professional?

Check out our website!

http://www.veryyoungprofessionals.com

www.ingramcontent.com/pod-product-compliance
Lightning Source LLC
LaVergne TN
LVHW071029070426
835507LV00002B/87